REEN IS NOT ONE COLOUR ON CAMELS LISTEN

IEW NORMAL THIS IS HOW THE CHANGE IN

G TO MUSIC CLIMATE OR W OIO

REEN IS NOT ONE COLOUR II

IEW NORMAL THIS IS HOW CHANGE BEGIN

G TO MUSIC CLIMATE OR WEATHER IT'S A CHOIO

REEN IS NOT ONE COLOUR ON CAMELS LISTENI

IEW NORMAL THIS IS HOW THE CHANGE BEGIN

G TO MUSIC CLIMATE OR WEATHER IT'S A CHOIO

REEN IS NOT ONE COLOUR ON CAMELS LISTENI

IEW NORMAL THIS IS HOW THE CHANGE BEGIN

G TO MUSIC CLIMATE OR WEATHER IT'S A CHOIO

REEN IS NOT ONE COLOUR ON CAMELS LISTENI

IEW NORMAL THIS IS HOW THE CHANGE BEGIN

G TO MUSIC CLIMATE OR WEATHER IT'S A CHOIO

REEN IS NOT ONE COLOUR ON CAMELS LISTENI

IEW NORMAL THIS IS HOW THE CHANGE BEGIN

G TO MUSIC CLIMATE OR WEATHER IT'S A CHOIO

REEN IS NOT ONE COLOUR ON CAMELS LISTENI

IEW NORMAL THIS IS HOW THE CHANGE BEGIN

G TO MUSIC CLIMATE OR W OIO

REEN IS NOT ONE COLOUR

C000024385

This is How the Change Begins
Published in Great Britain in 2021
by Graffeg Limited.

Written by Nicola Davies copyright
© 2021. Designed and produced by
Graffeg Limited copyright © 2021.

Graffeg Limited, 15 Neptune Court,
Vanguard Way, Cardiff, CF24 5PJ,
Wales, UK. Tel 01554 824000.
www.graffeg.com.

The publisher acknowledges
the financial support of the
Books Council of Wales.
www.gwales.com.

ISBN 9781913634247

1 2 3 4 5 6 7 8 9

MIX
Paper from
responsible sources
FSC® C014138

THIS IS HOW THE CHANGE BEGINS

NICOLA DAVIES

GRAFFEG

CONTENTS

INTRODUCTION

The poems here were written for two different projects, *Weather Watchers* for the Natural Environment Research Council with Hay Festival and *Your Forest* for Wild Rumpus Festival. My thanks to both festivals and funding organisations, to interviewees and to my collaborator, climate scientist Prof. Ed Hawkins.

I know that poems alone won't bring about the changes we need right now. But imagination, dreams and the words that carry them are a start. That *is* how the change begins.

Nicola Davies

NEW
NORMAL

MAKE THE NIGHTINGALES SHUT UP

In nineteen twenty my dad chased

lapwing chicks across the common.

In the spring of nineteen forty

he fired his Lee Enfield into the woods,

to make the nightingales shut up.

MY KIDS DON'T KNOW

I didn't miss the nightingales I'd never heard

or wonder why I'd never seen a lapwing chick.

The same way my kids don't know

that you couldn't leave a window open

and a light on, in the sixties,

because the room would fill with moths.

DENUDED

Every year's a new, denuded normal,

a slow shutdown of life with

expectations lowered, lowered, lowered,

until all we see's our own feet

on the concrete pavement.

FLOCKS OF CLOUDS OF HERDS OF

We need to long for what we've
never even known:

for corncrakes in the crook of every field;

for woods that we get lost in;

for sudden clearings, crammed with flowers;

for swallows jostling for space on wires;

for wolf voices shivering the night;

for bears turning out the dustbins.

For flocks of, clouds of, herds of,

for nature abundant and strong and all around.

A STORM OF JOY

So I'll tell you about the dawn chorus,

so loud it woke me;

the green bush-crickets landing

on my bedroom wall;

the butterflies that flew in clouds from bushes

on suburban railway sidings,

and the flock of curlew that made a storm of joy

so great, inside my heart,

I thought I'd break.

THE LONGING AND THE LOSS

I'll tell you about the beauty
that clothed and populated every day,

so together we will feel the longing and the loss,

because that's the start.

THIS IS HOW THE CHANGE BEGINS

HEATWAVE IN THE ARCTIC

Little drops of water and little grains of sand,

make the mighty ocean and the promised land.

This is how the change begins.

With a heatwave in the Arctic

and New York under snow

and a little mountain pika

with no place left to go.

This is how

This is how

This is how the change begins

OUR
FAULT

With an island in the ocean

where fresh water's turned to salt

and an oil company executive

who says it's not our fault.

This is how

This is how

This is how the change begins

DENIALS FED BY FEAR

With the permafrost that's melting

and with coral bleached to white,

with animals once plentiful

that vanish overnight,

with selfishness and greed and lies

denials fed by fear,

while storms and droughts and famines

grow with every passing year.

This is how

This is how

This is how the change begins

ACT ON TRUTH

With windmills on the hilltops

and solar panels on the roof.

With governments and businesses,

that finally act on truth.

By seeing that our future

can be better than our past,

and that the century that's coming

doesn't have to be our last.

A WORLD THAT'S TRULY GREEN

By learning how to share, not own,

by remembering to dream

of a world that's kinder, fairer,

a world that's truly green.

We are but drops of water,

we are but grains of sand,

but together we're an ocean

we can make a promised land!

This is how

This is how

This is how the change begins

GREEN IS NOT ONE COLOUR

FIST
OF FERN
BEFORE
UNFURLING

Green is not one colour.

It is beech leaves in early May

the fist of fern before unfurling.

UNBLOOMED

It is a hillside when the sun slips below the cloud

for one last burst,

a pine tree's aura in the dusk, at distance.

It is unbloomed tulips in the park,

bramble thorns and the inside of an acorn's cup.

THE HILL'S SUMMIT

It is the grass wrapped by a cow's tongue

and dusty nettles.

It is the short-cropped cliff-top sward,

the tooth-leafed dandelion

biting at the concrete's edge,

the hill's summit.

IT IS YOURS

It is not white,

it is not owned,

but it is yours.

ON CAMELS LISTENING TO MUSIC

EARTH
RAINBOWS
MOONLIGHT

The genius Alhazen,

whose name is Hasan Ibn al-Haytham,

whose *nisba* is al-Basri,

pondered many things:

the configuration of the earth;

rainbows; moonlight;

the way the world jinks between

the left eye and the right;

if camels can be induced to change

their pace, by music.

PRISM
OF THE
ATMOSPHERE

And dusk, when light lingers,

though the sun is gone,

shining through the prism

of the atmosphere,

to turn the Nile,

to brass and copper,

before darkness and the proper night,

Alhazen timed the twilight,

used the sun's angular progression for calibration,

and, by geometry, gave us the thickness

of the atmosphere.

FLIMSY FRAGILE PRECIOUS

A figure pretty close to the one that we know now:

fifty miles.

It sounds a lot, until you're en route to the moon,

and then the earth's an orange and the

atmosphere a sheet of clingfilm,

a flimsy, fragile, precious veil,

a swirl of blue and white,

the fingerprint of life

against the empty black of space.

FOOTPRINT

Look up now and feel it,

that fifty miles of air above your head.

Stretch out your arms and hold a column of it,

teetering on a base just like a picnic table.

That see-through Lego tower of gas is all yours.

It is the co^2 that all you do,

and are, results in every year.

Your carbon footprint.

DUSTY GOLD
OF TWILIGHT

Open both your eyes and ponder on it,

on the orange and the clingfilm.

On the dusty gold of twilight, rainbows, moonlight,

and camels listening to music by the Nile.

CLIMATE
OR
WEATHER

THE WEATHER BLOWS THE MARQUEE CLEAN AWAY

Climate makes you book the wedding for late May,

Order smoked salmon, champagne, all the frills.

Then weather blows the marquee clean away

And all your guests head home with chills.

SOMETHING'S GOING ON

The barbecue that got rained off at six?

The fog that made all Thameslink trains run late?

The match, scrapped 'cos of a frozen pitch?

That's weather, that's what that is, mate!

But when the ski resort at last goes bust,

Because in seven winters no snow fell.

Or when the garden and the orchard turn to dust,

Because the water table fell below the well.

That's when you know that something's going on.

That's when you know the climate has gone wrong.

IT'S A CHOICE

WE DON'T HAVE TO
GIVE UP
HOPE

It isn't a done deal.

We don't have to give up hope.

We can change our own behaviour,

we can throw ourselves a rope.

The future doesn't have to be a

wasteland filled with sorrow.

Act today to change the way the world

will be tomorrow.

We've all to gain and much, much,

more than everything to lose.

So look carefully in the mirror,

and tell yourself,

choose.

NOTES

NEW NORMAL

Maya Rose Craig, ornithologist and activist, was interviewed for the *Your Forest* project. She spoke eloquently about having a higher aspiration for conservation in the UK; not just returning to the denied baseline of 20 or even 30 years ago but to the richness of the pre-Industrial Revolution countryside.

THIS IS HOW THE CHANGE BEGINS

Climate change is happening now. It's not something that's in the future. The signs are everywhere, in changing weather patterns and the distribution of species of living things. How it will affect all our lives depends on how fast human behaviour can change to do everything we do differently.

GREEN IS NOT ONE COLOUR

Rhiane Fatinikun is the inspirational founder of Black Girls Hike, which encourages women and girls of colour to get out into the countryside. I was shocked to hear how unwelcome many people of colour are made to feel in the UK countryside.

Nature belongs to no one, green is everyone's colour.

ON CAMELS LISTENING TO MUSIC

The mathematician and thinker Hasan Ibn al-Haytham, known as Alhazen, or 'The Second Ptolemy', lived across the junction of the 10th and 11th centuries. He was the first person to measure the thickness of our atmosphere. His estimate of 50 miles is close to measurements made today.

CLIMATE OR WEATHER

Understanding why a 1.5 degree rise in global temperatures matters depends on understanding the difference between climate and weather. For someone untrained in science or statistics this is tricky, and few communicators seem to address it. I wrote this to help out.

IT'S A CHOICE

We are walking close to the edge of disaster; there's no doubt that climate change could end human civilisation. But it doesn't have to. We have all the tools we need, all we lack is the collective will to change. So, as Ghandi said, **'Be the change'.**